Table of Contents

What Are Fractions? 4
Working with Fractions 12
Glossary 22
To Learn More 23
Index 24

What Are Fractions?

My five friends and I are having a pizza party! There are eight equal slices.

÷ FUN + WITH − MATH ×

Fractions

by Janie Scheffer

BLASTOFF! 2 READERS

BLASTOFF! READERS, AN IMPRINT OF BELLWETHER MEDIA BY FLUTTERBEE

Blastoff! Readers are carefully developed by literacy experts to build reading stamina and move students toward fluency by combining standards-based content with developmentally appropriate text.

Level 1 provides the most support through repetition of high-frequency words, light text, predictable sentence patterns, and strong visual support.

Level 2 offers early readers a bit more challenge through varied sentences, increased text load, and text-supportive special features.

Level 3 advances early-fluent readers toward fluency through increased text load, less reliance on photos, advancing concepts, longer sentences, and more complex special features.

★ **Blastoff! Universe**

This edition first published in 2027 by Bellwether Media, Inc.

For information regarding permission, write to Bellwether Media, Inc., Attention: Permissions Department, 3500 American Blvd W, Suite 150, Bloomington, MN 55431.

Library of Congress Cataloging-in-Publication Data

Names: Scheffer, Janie, 1992- author
Title: Fractions / by Janie Scheffer.
Description: Minneapolis, Minnesota : Bellwether Media, Inc., 2027. | Series: Fun with math | Includes bibliographical references and index. | Audience: Ages 5-8 | Audience: Grades 2-3 | Summary: "Relevant images match informative text in this introduction to fractions. Intended for students in kindergarten through third grade"-- Provided by publisher.
Identifiers: LCCN 2026011067 (print) | LCCN 2026011068 (ebook) | ISBN 9798898800543 library binding | ISBN 9798898802950 paperback | ISBN 9798898801786 ebook
Subjects: LCSH: Fractions | Mathematics
Classification: LCC QA117 .S33 2027 (print) | LCC QA117 (ebook)
LC record available at https://lccn.loc.gov/2026011067
LC ebook record available at https://lccn.loc.gov/2026011068

Editor: Rebecca Sabelko   Designer: Brittany McIntosh

Printed in the United States of America, North Mankato, MN.

We each get one slice. How much of the pizza will we eat?

How Much Pizza Will We Eat?

See answer on page 23!

Fractions show parts of a whole.
Each part is equal.

$\frac{5}{6}$ have sprinkles

Fractions have a top number and a bottom number.

The top number is the **numerator**. It is the number of parts taken from the whole.

The bottom number is the **denominator**. It is the total number of equal parts.

numerator

$$\frac{1}{6}$$

denominator

1/8
1/8
1/8
1/8
1/8
1/8
1/8
1/10
1/10
1/10
1/10
1/10
1/3
1/6
1/6
1/6
1/6
1/4

Proper fractions show numbers that are less than one whole.

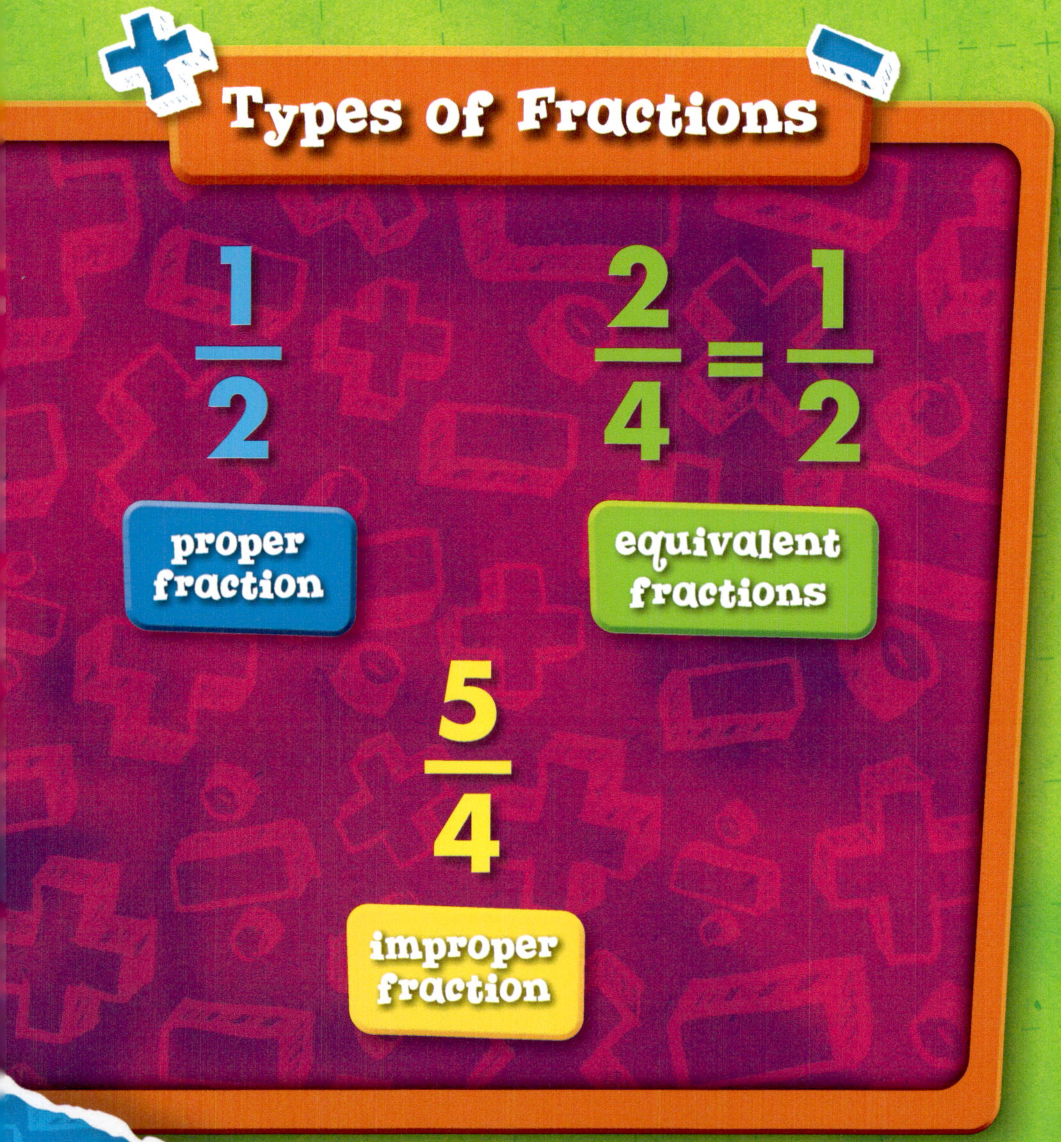

Equivalent fractions show the same **value** when they are **simplified**. Fractions that show numbers that are more than one whole are **improper fractions**.

Working with Fractions

Fractions help people work with numbers in more exact ways.

Fractions help people measure things.

2 1/2
20 OZ
2 1/3
2 CUPS
16
2 CUPS
1 2/3
1 1/2
12
1 1/3
1 CUP
8
1 CUP
2/3
1/2
4

measuring cups

People use fractions to cook and bake. Measuring cups help people use exact amounts of **ingredients**.

People use fractions to share. Food can be cut into equal pieces.

Fractions help find exact measurements. People use tape measures that show exact **units**.

Fractions help people count money. People may need less than one dollar. They use **coins**.

People use fractions to track time in sports. Some games have **periods**.

People use fractions to tell time. People may say 30 minutes is a half hour.

Fractions help us understand parts of a whole.

They are an important part of everyday life!

Glossary

coins—pieces of metal money that are small, flat, and round

denominator—the bottom number in a fraction

equivalent fractions—fractions that are the same value or equal

improper fractions—fractions in which the numerator is greater than the denominator

ingredients—foods that are part of a recipe

numerator—the top number in a fraction

periods—timed parts of sports games, such as quarters or halves, with short breaks in between

proper fractions—fractions in which the numerator is less than the denominator

simplified—broken down to be the most basic form of a fraction

units—amounts or items used in measurements

value—the worth or importance of something

To Learn More

AT THE LIBRARY

Davis, Bela. *Break It Up!: Sharing with Fractions.* Minneapolis, Minn.: Abdo Kids Junior, 2025.

Scheffer, Janie. *Graphs.* Minneapolis, Minn.: Bellwether Media, 2027.

Wise, Bill. *The Cake Problem: Equivalent and Simplified Fractions.* New York, N.Y.: Clavis, 2025.

ON THE WEB

FACTSURFER

Factsurfer.com gives you a safe, fun way to find more information.

1. Go to www.factsurfer.com.
2. Enter "fractions" into the search box and click 🔍.
3. Select your book cover to see a list of related content.

The answer to the question on page 5 is $\frac{6}{8}$ or $\frac{3}{4}$!

Index

denominator, 8
food, 4, 5, 15
measuring cups, 14
money, 17
numerator, 8
sports, 18
tape measures, 16
telling time, 19
types of fractions, 10, 11

The images in this book are reproduced through the courtesy of: YesPhotographers, front cover; Pixel-Shot, p. 3; Monkey Business Images, p. 4; Aytana Mayotte, p. 5; Erhan Inga, p. 6; Lazy_Bear, p. 7; Halfpoint, pp. 8-9; BublikHaus, p. 11; JoshBryan, p. 12; Christy Thompson, pp. 12-13; wavebreak3, p. 14; WhitePlaid, p. 14 (inset); SergeyCo, p. 15; New Africa, p. 16; Natee Meepian, p. 17; Solomon Thompson, p. 18; Eric, p. 18 (inset); olga chuprina, p. 19; Sukjai Photo, p. 20; Shebeko, pp. 20-21; Moiz Contributor 8002, p. 22.